The Innovative Sch
Leader's Guide to

social
media

recruit students, engage parents,
and share your school's story

Dr. Brian J. Dixon

The Innovative School Leader's Guide to Using Social Media

Dr. Brian J. Dixon

Thank you to the students, parents, and faculty of Mentorship Academy, who help make our school story one worthy of telling.

Special thanks to Kelley McCormick who helped us get started..

Table of Contents

Introduction

Our world has changed. In an age of Facebook and Twitter, your school community expects more than just open houses and photocopied newsletters. They want frequent updates, they want to give their feedback, they expect to be part of a collaborative community. This guide will show you the basics of many of today's most popular social media tools to help you engage your target audience, communicate the mission and vision of your school, serve as another resource in your student recruitment strategy, and inspire business and community involvement.

What is Social Media?

Social media is the use of web-based technologies to turn communication into interactive dialogue. A key component of social media is the creation and exchange of user-generated content. Students and teachers savvy in social media create and exchange original content constantly, enhancing the educational conversations occurring throughout the school community.

Reasons to use Social Media

There are many reasons to use social media including:

Engaged Families - Keep your school community "in the loop" by sharing events and updates through social media such as Facebook and Twitter. Receive feedback through comments, email, and online surveys. These tools allow you to keep families engaged in a continuous conversation about your school. Families that have a connection with your school will advocate for your school and aid in your grassroots marketing efforts.

Larger Events - Create greater parent and community awareness for your events. Start communicating information about your events using social media and you'll see event participation increase.

Authentic Feedback - Social Media gives you the opportunity to monitor what is being said about your school and participate in the conversation.

Fundraising - Engaging potential donors starts with telling your school's story. Social media is a great way to give donors a glimpse into your organization and hear your story, help donors get to know your school and learn about opportunities to participate.

Community Buy-in - Social Media allows you to build relationships with community members by including them in the conversation, creating more advocates and partners for your organization.

Student recruitment/enrollment - Seeing their work displayed on your Social Media can help to create ownership and excitement among your students. Displaying student work in this way also helps you begin a conversation with potential students, offering an inside glimpse into your school, helping them make a more informed decision when choosing between your school and another.

Leading the conversation

Become a thought leader in your area by frequently using social media. Seeing your school on Facebook and YouTube will add both credibility and personality to your school in the minds of your students, parents, and community members. What you post on your Social Media pages will impact the conversation taking place at other educational institutions in your area.

Familiar tools, innovative uses

Your target audience already uses many of social media tools. Families are watching online videos for their nightly entertainment. Students use Facebook to stay in touch with their friends. And more and more businesses are discovering Twitter. These three tools alone can radically impact the community's perception of your school in positive ways.

What to expect from this book

What you will find in these next few chapters are real-life, practical examples from our website and other social media platforms. We share the lessons we've learned as well as tips and tricks we have implemented along the way. Now let's get started.   5

E-newsletters

Email newsletters are a cost-effective way to regularly communicate school events and news with parents, community members and donors. An e-newsletter program allows you to use templates, customize newsletters, add social media links, and track who views, opens, and forwards your e-newsletter.

Advantages of E-newsletter services

E-newsletter services, such as MyEmma.com, iContact, and Constant Contact, walk you step-by-step through the newsletter creation process. These services make your e-newsletter strategy simple with tools for design, contact management, user tracking, newsletter archiving, and collecting email addresses.

Design tools

E-newsletter services provide professionally designed templates you can customize. With simple drag and drop features, creating an attractive email is pretty easy. You can also reuse and repurpose previously sent emails by simply updating the content for a new mailing, saving you design time.

Contact management

Target each of your audiences by using the contact management features. Start by uploading your email database as a custom lit, categorizing your audiences as parents, students, community volunteers, and potential teachers. These email services allow you to easily upload and organize your contacts into many custom lists. Target each group individually with a message that is relevant to them and choose which list will receive that particular message. Each e-newsletter we send is written to meet the needs of a specific target audience.

Date Sent ▾	Email Name	Sent	Bounces	Spam Reports	Opt-outs	Opens	Clicks	Forwards
11/1/2010	Nov. 1st update	156	2.6% (4)	0	0	21.1% (32)	9.4% (3)	0
10/21/2010	October Newsletter	420	4.3% (18)	0	0.7% (3)	27.9% (112)	0.9% (1)	0
7/20/2010	Mentorship Academy Parental Advisory Council	177	4.0% (7)	0	0.6% (1)	37.6% (64)	0	0

User tracking

E-newsletter services also allow you to track several key components when sending your email including:
-how many people opened the e-newsletter
-what links users clicked on in your email
-how many emails were "bounced" or not received
-how many people unsubscribed from your list

Understanding how your audience interacts with your e-newsletter based on this data tracking is a powerful tool for engaging your school community.

Newsletter archive

Constant Contact also allows you to post e-newsletters directly to your website and social media platforms. This is a great way to share your e-newsletter content with those who are not on your email list.

Collect email addresses

Ensure that every visitor to your site is invited to sign up for your e-newsletter. Collecting these email addresses allows us to continue the conversation with visitors once they have left our site. First time visitors to our site are directed to a special landing page featuring a high-definition video and e-newsletter sign-up. After receiving this introductory information, visitors are forwarded to our comprehensive website.

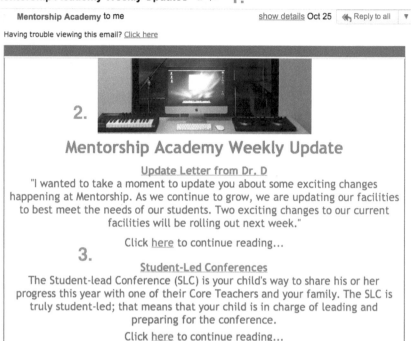

Mentorship Academy to me   show details Oct 25   ↰ Reply to all   ▼

Having trouble viewing this email? Click here

2.

Mentorship Academy Weekly Update

Update Letter from Dr. D
"I wanted to take a moment to update you about some exciting changes happening at Mentorship. As we continue to grow, we are updating our facilities to best meet the needs of our students. Two exciting changes to our current facilities will be rolling out next week."

Click here to continue reading...

3.

Student-Led Conferences
The Student-lead Conference (SLC) is your child's way to share his or her progress this year with one of their Core Teachers and your family. The SLC is truly student-led; that means that your child is in charge of leading and preparing for the conference.

Click here to continue reading...

Join Our Mailing List!

Follow us on **twitter**   Find us on **Facebook** 🗗

Mentorship Academy
339 Florida St.
Baton Rouge, Louisiana 70801
225-346-5180

Forward email   **5.**

✉ SafeUnsubscribe®   Email Marketing by
This email was sent to info@mentorshipacademy.org by kmccormick@mentorshipacademy.
org.
Update Profile/Email Address | Instant removal with SafeUnsubscribe™ | Privacy Policy.   *Constant Contact*
                                                                          TRY IT FREE
Mentorship Academy | 339 Florida St. | Baton Rouge | LA | 70801

1. Email subject line - Make it something your audience will want to open.

2. Picture - Use the first section of your newsletter to grab your audience's attention with a relevant picture.

3. Article - Highlight key events, feature updates, and remind parents of your mission through timely articles.

4. Contact info - This section features our social media links, address, and contact info for easy linking and access.

5. Safe unsubscribe - Ensure you are complying with anti-spam laws by using the built in unsubscribe features.

E-newsletters

Content is key

The most important aspect of your e-newsletter strategy is writing and sharing great content. Make sure you have something to say and a reason to send it to your target audience. We use e-newsletters to share weekly updates, send parent reminders, recruit faculty, and plan events.

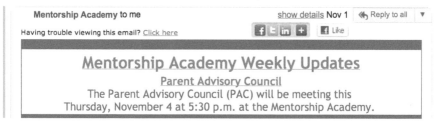

| Mentorship Academy to me | show details 10/19/10 ⤺ Reply to all ▼ |

Mentorship Academy Weekly Update
Mentorship Academy Fall Formal
The Mentorship Academy Fall Formal will take place
Friday, October 29 from 8-10 p.m.
at the Shaw Center for the Arts' 4th floor River Terrace.

Weekly Updates:
To keep our school community engaged and updated, we send out the Mentorship Academy Weekly Updates. This email highlights the incredible opportunities, projects and partnerships taking place at our school. There is also a Teacher-Spotlight article where the school community can get to know one of our faculty members on a more personal level.

| Mentorship Academy to me | show details Nov 1 ⤺ Reply to all ▼ |
| Having trouble viewing this email? Click here | f t in + ☐ Like |

Mentorship Academy Weekly Updates
Parent Advisory Council
The Parent Advisory Council (PAC) will be meeting this
Thursday, November 4 at 5:30 p.m. at the Mentorship Academy.

Parent Reminders:
Announcements about upcoming events and the notes from each Parental Advisory Council meeting are sent out via e-newsletter to all of the parents on our parent contact list at the beginning of every week. Parent email addresses are both collected at the beginning of the year and updated frequently with the help of the teachers. Getting correct parent email addresses is essential to communicating with this vital target audience.

Teacher recruiting:
Beginning each January we host recruiting events for the hiring of next year's teaching staff. We create and distribute a custom e-newsletter for these potential teachers, keeping them engaged, informed and excited about our school and the hiring process. Using our e-newsletters in this way helps us create a qualified pool of applicants to choose from when we start making hiring decisions.

9

Event planning with Constant Contact

Constant Contact an essential tool for hosting events and conferences. Features such as a signup form, template for event announcements, survey tools, and a process for purchasing tickets online help us manage our events. We use Constant Contact as one of the key tools in the marketing of our annual Project-based Learning Summit conference. Attendees can register for the conference through the e-newsletter and purchase their tickets in one convenient place.

When
Saturday February 27, 2010 from 9:00 AM to 2:00 PM
Where
Manship Theatre
100 Lafayette St.
Baton Rouge, LA 70801

Project Based Learning Summit

Event Marketing by
Constant Contact
TRY IT FREE

Personal Information

* First Name:
* Last Name:
* Email Address:

Register   Close Window

Event guests are able to register online with a simple form.

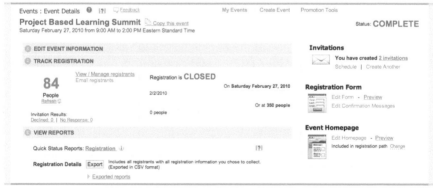

Track registrants, invitations, and details using Constant Contact.

E-newsletters

Constant Contact Overview

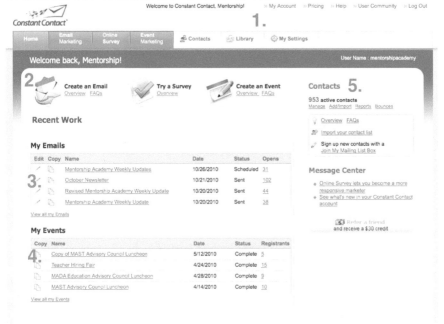

1. Main Dashboard - This section allows you to access contacts, settings, and other account details.

2. Action area - Create a new email, make a survey, or create an event using this section.

3. My Emails - Edit, copy, and review the statistics on recent emails you've created and sent out.

4. My Events - This section allows you to update information on your school's events.

5. Contacts - Manage, import, or review your list of email contacts.

Training resources

A final benefit of using a service like Constant Contact is the wealth of training resources available. YouTube hosts thousands of training videos. The Constant Contact User Community helps newcomers and experienced users get their questions answered through crowdsourcing. Finally, many cities host regular in-person training seminars for Constant Contact.

Facebook

Facebook is the world's most popular social networking site. With over 500 million users, if you want to build your school's reputation in the community, you must have a presence on Facebook. Two main ways to use Facebook to engage your community is your Facebook fan page and Facebook ads.

Facebook fan page

Unlike the standard personal Facebook account, businesses and nonprofits can create a "fan page" to establish a presence on Facebook. Our fan page is where we post contact information, school updates, and multimedia content. Creating a Facebook "Fan" Page is a great way to keep your community updated on your school in a place they check regularly.

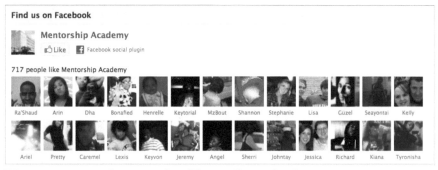

Keys to a dynamic Facebook fan page:

1. Post new content everyday - By updating our page at least twice a day we can engage our fans in a daily conversation. Sharing the responsibility of posting updates among several faculty members helps keep the content interesting.

2. Keep it fun and positive - Facebook is focused on connecting users with friends and family. Keeping your page fund and positive will help your school benefit from the familiarity people experience on Facebook.

3. Relevant information - Consider what your Facebook fans would want to know about your school. Relevant information such as an event reminder, a link to a permission form, or schedule update will ensure your fans find the content you post valuable to them.

4. Media rich experience - Photos and videos are powerful means to tell your school's story. Posting media frequently keeps your fans interested in your school and encourages them to visit your page frequently.

Facebook Overview

1. Your profile icon - This should be your school logo or a photo that is easily connected to your school such as your school building or mascot.

2. Full name - Your full school name goes here.

3. Short bio - You only have a few sentences to describe your school in this bio section, so focus on the most important key words.

4. Contact information - Address, phone number, and office hours go here.

5. Status Update Box - This is where you enter new posts, upload photos, videos, links and add new events. Anything that you would like your target audiences to know should be placed here.

6&7. Recent Updates - This section of your Facebook "Wall" features recent updates including events, links, and photos.

Example Facebook Posts

There are many types of information you can post on your Facebook page. As you can see below, we have used our page to post event information, school reminders, pictures and highlights, and to answer questions.

Event information:
Our Facebook page is a great place to post event information.

 Mentorship Academy Fall Formal tickets are on sale now through Friday, October 29! Tickets are $8. The Fall Formal will be Friday, Oct. 29 from 8–10 p.m. at the Shaw Center for the Arts.

P October 26 at 3:09pm via Ping.fm · Comment · Like · Share · Promote

👍 Ximena Mejiia likes this.

 Event details can be posted on Facebook.|

Comment

School reminders:
Since so many people check Facebook everyday, it is a central place to post reminders of upcoming dates, permission slips, and announcements.

 Mentorship Academy Parents: Please be reminded that the school will be closed on Election Day, Tuesday, November 2nd.

14 hours ago · Comment · Like · Share · Promote

👍 7 people like this.

 Facebook is a great place to post reminders.|

Comment

Pictures and highlights:
Everything new and innovative we do is added to our Facebook page. Posting pictures and video on Facebook helps your target audience get to know your school in an authentic way.

 Mentorship Academy

Fitness Studio & Multimedia Lab
19 new photos

📷 October 26 at 11:36am · Comment · Like · Share

Answer questions:

Facebook is a two-way conversation allowing direct responses to parents and students in real time.

 Mentorship Academy Read about all of the innovative things happening at the #MentorshipAcademies in our October newsletter!

 Updates from the Mentorship Academies
conta.cc

October 21 at 4:00pm · Comment · Like · Share · Promote

👍 2 people like this.

 Meredith Kwentua where can we find the newsletter
October 21 at 7:23pm · Like · Flag

 Mentorship Academy Just click on this link:
http://conta.cc/dkOdsr
a few seconds ago · Like

 Erica Ladii Martin What is the website to check the students grades?
October 28 at 8:42pm · Comment · Like

 Mentorship Academy Engrade.com
October 29 at 3:07pm · Like

Managing your Facebook account:

You can make multiple users administrators on your Facebook account. Even when I am logged onto my personal Facebook, I can post on Mentorship Academy's Wall as "Mentorship Academy". (For an example see the above responses.) This way, you do not have to log out as yourself and log in as your school, you can manage both personal and business from one account.

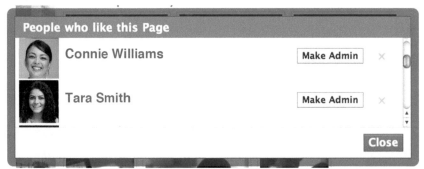

Make multiple users your Facebook administrators.

Facebook Ads Overview

A feature of Facebook you may not have considered are "Pay per Click" advertisements. For just a few dollars, you can create an ad campaign on Facebook to target a specific demographic of users. Not only is this a very unique way to get your audience's attention, but it is an invaluable method for recruiting future students and teachers.

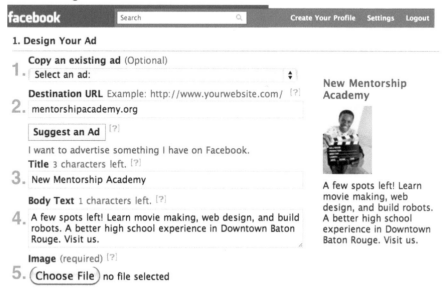

1. Copy an existing ad - You can reuse elements of previous ads to continually improve your ad or test the success rate of different ads.

2. Destination URL - This is the "landing page" where visitors are led after they click on your ad. You can link to a video, your website, or to a form to collect their email address and add them to your e-newsletter list.

3. Title - Write a clear, attention-grabbing title. Be specific about what you are offering or you will end up paying for clicks by visitors who aren't part of your target audience.

4. Body Text - Now that you have the viewer's attention, you have just a few words to convince them to click. Use your keywords here and a "call to action" to ensure they click for more information. We use action phrases like "learn movie making," "build robots," and "visit us" to entice visitors to click on our ad to learn more about our school.

5. Image - You only have a small picture to get your audience's attention. Instead of a logo or picture of the school, we used a stock photo of a student actually making a movie. The picture is the first element of your ad that visitors will notice, so balance grabbing their attention with a photo that best relates to them and represents your school.

2. Targeting   Ad Targeting FAQ

Location Country: [?]

United States ×

○ Everywhere
○ By State/Province [?]
◉ By City [?]

Baton Rouge, LA ×

☑ Include cities within | 10 ⬍ | miles.

Demographics

Age: [?] | Any ⬍ | – | 15 ⬍ |
                  ☐ Require exact age match [?]

Sex: [?]   ◉ All   ○ Men   ○ Women

Likes & Interests

Science ×	[?]

Connections on Facebook

Connections: [?]   Target users who are connected to:

Enter your Page, Event, Group, or Application	[?]

                   Target users who are not already connected to:

Mentorship Academy ×	[?]

Friends of   Target users whose friends are connected to:
connections:

Enter your Page, Event, Group, or Application	[?]

⊞ Show Advanced Targeting Options

Estimated Reach

2,740 people

- who live in the **United States**
- who live within 10 miles of **Baton Rouge, LA**
- **15** years old and younger
- who like **science**
- who are not already connected to **Mentorship Academy**

Targeting your ad

Facebook allows you to be very selective about who sees your ad, ensuring that you only pay to advertise to members of your target audience. The above screenshot shows how narrow you can focus your ad, from geographic location and age to likes and interests.

Facebook Ads Return on Investment

We used Facebook Ads to engage our target audience of upcoming 9th graders. Let's break down a day's worth of advertising using the chart below.

Daily stats for the week of: Jun 27 ▾

Date	Imp.	Social %	Clicks	CTR (%)	Avg. CPC ($)	Avg. CPM ($)	Spent ($)
07/01/2010	241,622	58.2%	93	0.04	0.52	0.20	48.34
06/30/2010	236,340	57.1%	94	0.04	0.51	0.20	47.98
06/29/2010	213,689	56.7%	81	0.04	0.52	0.20	42.24
Lifetime	2,802,219	56.2%	1,122	0.04	0.50	0.20	557.76

Date - The 24 hour period the ad was run. For this breakdown, we'll focus on July 1st, the highlighted section above.

Impressions - The number of times our ad was displayed on the screen of a member of our target audience. On July 1st, our ad was displayed **241,622** times. This is the number of times an ad appears on a page, whether or not the viewer noticed it. The clicks are what count.

Social % - The percent of impressions where the ad was shown with information about a viewer's friend who connected to our page. Our Social percentage was **58.2%**. This means that over half of our ads were tied to a social connection, increasing the trust factor of our ads.

Clicks - Clicks are counted each time a user clicks through your ad to your landing page. Our ad was clicked on **93** times. This number is the key towards measuring your ad's success.

Click Through Rate (CTR) - Click-through rate (CTR) is the number of clicks your ad receives divided by the number of times your ad is shown on the site (impressions) in the same time period. Our click-through rate was **.04%**, meaning that a small fraction of people who saw the ad, clicked on it.

Average Cost Per Click (CPC) - This is the amount you're paying on average for each click on your ad. This is calculated as: total clicks on your ad / cost for that ad during the same time period = average CPC. Our CPC was **$0.52**, meaning that it costs half a dollar for each person who clicked on our ad.

Average Cost Per Thousand (CPM) - This is the amount you're paying on average for every thousand impressions (views) of your ad. This number is less relevant than Cost Per Click.

Spent - This is the total amount we spent for one day of advertising on Facebook. For **$48.34**, our ad appeared **241,622** times and was clicked on **93** times.

Our landing page

Viewers that clicked on our ad were directed to the below landing page where they watched an overview video about our school and could sign up for our email newsletter.

Although we used traditional media such as the local news, student recruitment events, face-to-face presentations, billboards, and mail out postcards, the best use of our money was our Facebook ads. The average billboard costs $1000 a month. Imagine how much further these dollars could go with a specifically targeted Facebook ad campaign.

Twitter

Twitter allows you to post "status updates", with "Tweets" answering the question "What are you doing now?". Schools constantly have news and events worth sharing with the larger community. Twitter is a great tool to share these updates with the tech-savvy members of your community.

What should you tweet?

Reminders - Anything that you need your students and/or families to remember such as field trip permission slips, back to school night, school holidays, and survey reminders are all valid topics for Twitter.

Upcoming Events - Hosting an event? Start tweeting early with a hash tag (#) representing the event. Those interested in your event can search for your topic. Our school hosts a Project-based Learning Summit with the hashtag #pblsummit. We tweet out this tag often before and during the conference. This helps to keep the conversation organized and links all participants together. Anytime someone tweets about the event using your hashtag, you can see what has been said.

Survey Questions - You can tweet out a question and get instant feedback from your followers. You could also send out a link to an online survey you've created on Survey Monkey or Wufoo. Receiving authentic feedback allows you to continuously improve your communication and engage your target audiences.

Direct Outreach- Use the @reply tag to make direct contact with another Twitter user. This is also another way to contact local media, authors or even celebrities to share great news or get coverage of events happening at your school.

Example Tweets

When our school was featured on the local news, we sent out a tweet reminding our followers of the time to watch:

mentorshipbr Mentorship Academy
Watch student and staff interviews on NBC 33 at 5:00 P.M. and 10:00 P.M.
15 Oct ☆ Favorite ↩ Reply 🗑 Delete

We also use Twitter to direct followers to an online version of our weekly parent newsletter.

mentorshipbr Mentorship Academy
Click the link below to read our Weekly Updates Newsletter.
http://fb.me/zIaXkSP7
11 Oct ☆ Favorite ↩ Reply 🗑 Delete

We use Twitter to remind our parents about events, including our parental advisory council meetings.

mentorshipbr Mentorship Academy
Parent Advisory Council (PAC) meeting tonight at 6 p.m. at the school... You don't want to miss it!! Great time to...
http://fb.me/sM9qV5is
7 Oct ☆ Favorite ↩ Reply 🗑 Delete

Why use Twitter?

Easy to use - You can update Twitter from any Internet connected computer or cell phone. Sending out status updates or "tweets" is as simple as typing a short sentence.

Multiple platforms - Anyone following you on Twitter can access your updates from anywhere. Twitter also links easily to your Facebook page and other social media sites.

Simple sharing - Retweeting, when a follower forwards your message to his or her own followers, is standard practice on Twitter. When your update is "retweeted", other users on Twitter will see what you've posted and may choose to follow your school.

Getting started using Twitter

1. Sign up for an account - Just visit twitter.com and sign up. You'll start by choosing your Twitter username. Pick something that represents your school. Keep it short and be sure it follows your marketing and branding strategy.

2. Customize your profile - Followers who want to learn more about your school will start by visiting your Twitter profile. Customize elements such as your profile icon, background, and keyword to take advantage of their visit.

3. Follow other tweeters - Search for other twitter users in your field. Usually those who you follow, end up following you.

4. Start tweeting - Type a sentence or two giving an update on your school. Continue the practice and soon enough, people will start following you and reading your tweets.

Setting up your account:

2.**Mentorship Academy**

3.**@mentorshipbr** Baton Rouge, LA 6.

1.

4.*Project-based learning, technology-integration, and internship opportunities for Baton Rouge 9th graders. Mentorship Academy - connect, create, contribute*

5.http://www.mentorshipbr.org

1. Your profile icon - This should be your school logo or picture that is representative of your school.

2. Full name - Your full school name goes here.

3. Twitter handle - This is your username. It should be short, specific, and memorable.

4. Short bio - You only have a few characters to describe your school in this bio section so be sure to use the most important keywords.

5. Website - Include a link to your official school website so your followers can find out more about your organization and sign up for your e-newsletter.

6. Location - Type in your zip code to let followers know where you are located.

Our school's Twitter stats

Your homepage on Twitter, twitter.com/username, displays your Twitter statistics including the number of people following you, the number of people you are following, how many times you've tweeted, and any directories you are listed in.

 About @mentorshipbr

362	**422**	**260**	**4**
Tweets	Following	Followers	Listed

Following 422   Followers 260

Build your audience:

1. Follow local newsmakers - They'll likely follow you.

2. Follow national leaders - You'll be listed as a follower and others may check you out as a result.

3. Send direct messages - Ask specific questions of people you follow on twitter. They'll likely reply back to you.

 mentorshipbr Mentorship Academy
@leah600 We wanted to invite you out to visit the schools & speak to our students. Rt down the street at 339 Fla. How should we reach you?
11 Nov ☆ Favorite ↩ Reply ⅲ Delete

4. Start a conversation - Post tweets that encourage others to respond. Add your own # (hashmarks) to allow others to add to the conversation stream. The more people that engage in the conversation, the more you'll get your name out there.

 mentorshipbr Mentorship Academy
Tell us about your day and what you are learning on this Tuesday...
9 Nov ☆ Favorite ↩ Reply ⅲ Delete

School website

Begin with the audience in mind

Creating a school website that engages your audience is about more than just posting information about your school. You need to use your site to continuously participate in a conversation with your school community. Here is a step by step plan to follow:

1. Landing page

The first place your audience will visit is the landing page. This single page is a lot simpler than a traditional website, without any drop down menus or complex site navigation. Landing pages are also called "squeeze" pages, because users can only squeeze through one specific click to move on to the full site. Our landing page (see pg. 19) serves as a great introduction to our school, and includes graphics, a video overview, and an email signup. Users can then click on to our full website.

2. Finding information

Your school's website is the primary source of information about your school. It should be easy to navigate, fast-loading on even the slowest computers, frequently updated with relevant information, and visually appealing to positively represent your school's brand.

3. Information to include

Be sure the following information is easily accessible on your website:
1. school address, phone number, and driving directions
2. faculty pictures, email, and to classroom portals
3. e-newsletter signup (from Constant Contact)
4. social media links (including Facebook, Twitter, and YouTube)
5. important links for students and parents

4. Opportunities for engagement

Visitors to your site need to be invited to enter into a conversation with you. Strategies to begin this conversation include:
1. Signing up for the school e-newsletter
2. Following the school on Facebook and Twitter
3. Filling out a web form with a question or comment
4. Emailing a faculty member through the school's website

Our school website allows users the option to login when they visit the site, creating a personal experience for each user. This feature, enabled by the web-platform Joomla, allows users to view customized information according to their preferences.

1. Main menu - Your drop-down menu should be audience focused, allowing both web experts and beginners to easily navigate your site.

2. Current stories - Keep visitors coming back by featuring relevant stories with interesting pictures.

3. School information - Use the front page of your website to introduce your core principles to visitors. This helps set the tone for your site and gives visitors a better understanding of your school's philosophy.

4. Video - There should be at least one video on your homepage. Visitors are much more likely to watch a video than read text or view pictures.

5. Contact information - The school's phone number, address, and a link to driving directions should always be on your front page.

6. Social media links - Link all of your portals in one convenient place.

7. Email sign-up - Capture your visitors' email addresses to continue the conversation once they've left your site.

User-friendly platform

A five year old website no longer meets the needs of today's savvy web users. But it doesn't mean you have to start from scratch. The best websites take advantage of templates and modules to create a well designed, highly customizable web experience. Websites built on the joomla or wordpress platform allow you to choose from thousands of interesting templates. These platforms also allow school personnel to update their section of the website without effecting sections belonging to another department.

A mobile-friendly site

Your website will often be viewed on cell phones and other mobile devices. If your website is not iPhone or mobile friendly, it will be difficult for visitors to locate the address and phone number of your school while on the go. Test your site on multiple devices to ensure you have a site that works for all visitors.

School Website

Information central

Pack your website full of relevant, accessible information as it is the central point of communication for many members of your community. Be sure to include downloadable forms, archives of newsletters, and other information your community is asking for. Posting this info on your site will save you paper, time, and the headaches surrounding "take home packets". The Web has changed the way information is delivered by businesses and government, so consider how you might better share information with your school community.

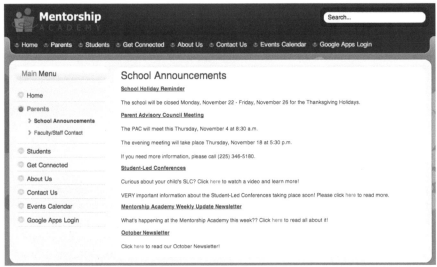

School announcements

We archive school announcements under the parent tab on our website for easy access later.

Social Media Links

Be sure to have links to your Social Media sites on the main page of your website. With one click, users will have access to your Facebook, Twitter and YouTube pages.

Ning

Building an online community

Ning.com is a customizable Facebook-like online application that features blogs, discussion forums, video sharing, and collaborative groups. Ning can be used effectively as a schoolwide collaborative network because the school administration controls who can use it, what features are enabled, and which content to approve. This level of management allows students the benefits of collaboration with added accountability that may be lacking on other sites.

A participatory school culture

Ning provides your school with an online portal for schoolwide collaboration. Community features such as blogs, discussion forums and poll questions help make this site a great tool for today's classroom. Having students complete and post their assignments on Ning gives teachers the ability to review student work and check for participation while allowing other students to view the contributions of their fellow classmates. Exemplary work can be featured on the front page to encourage and inspire the school community.

Managing inappropriate content

School administrators and parents often wonder what happens when a student posts an inappropriate comment or picture on the school's network. Ning provides two methods for dealing with this unwanted content. First, you can set up your Ning network to require that all content be approved by an administrator before that content is available online. Second, administrators are able to delete inappropriate content right on the Ning page with a single click. Both of these approaches help you identify the student posting the inappropriate content and begin to take the necessary steps. Effective steps include deleting posts, speaking with the student, involving parents, and banning the student from Ning for an appropriate length of time.

Measuring the school climate

Ning is also a great tool to help administrators understand the student experience at school via polling or a discussion prompt. Students can provide feedback through Ning, helping you continue to build a positive, collaborative school culture. Even if nothing can be done about the issue (buses, construction, testing, etc.) providing a forum where student voices can be heard is valuable to the overall school community.

a personalized collaborative network

1. Your school name - This is where your school name and motto go.

2. Notes - We use a notes module for important links our students need.

3. Members - This section allows you to access members' pages.

4. Forum - Forums allow members to discuss school related topics.

5. Blog Posts - This section features links to members' blog posts.

6. Content Approval - Administrators can moderate uploaded content here.

Student expression

Another aspect of Ning which makes it an interesting tool to use with today's students is personal expression. Although most schools block access to sites like Facebook, students need extensive training to deal with the new reality of social media. Ning allows students to build a profile as an outlet for personal expression, a means of interacting with their classmates and engaging in the course material- all within the monitored school context where they can learn safety and appropriateness.

Class discussions

Discussion forums are a great way to engage all of your students. An ongoing class discussion allows students to write and edit their posts before sharing with the class. Here is an example of a class discussion:

1. Discussion prompt - This is the question posted by the teacher.

2. Document attachments - Ning gives you the ability to attach documents to lead the discussion or to be used by the students for reference.

3. Admin options - This section allows the teacher a few management features including closing the discussion (if you want to establish a deadline), editing the discussion (if you want to refocus the topic), and add tags (so that the discussion can be found by searching Ning).

4. and 5. Replies to the Discussion - Responses are posted in descending order and display username, picture, and message. Students can reply to the larger topic or to a specific student response.

6. Follow discussion - Automatically receive an email notification when students reply to a specific discussion by "following" the discussion.

An online parent group

There are parents in your school community that are not able to attend your parent meetings on a regular basis. With this in mind, create a parent group on Ning for parents to ask questions, collaborate with other parents and participate in the school community.

A parent group is another place to post announcements and upcoming events that parents should be aware of. You can even make on of the parents the group moderator.

Another advantage of having your student's parents on Ning is the additional monitoring of student activity. By using Ning, parents will be able to view student work and participate in encouraging positive contributions.

Encouraging participation

Online social networks are becoming familiar territory for even the most technophobic parents. By making your parent group on Ning an essential hub for parental engagement, you'll begin to see more parents posting comments, suggestions, and helping to coordinate events within your school community.

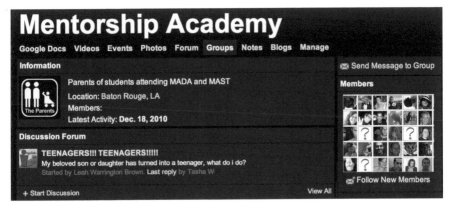

Mentorship Academy

Google Docs   Videos   Events   Photos   Forum   **Groups**   Notes   Blogs   Manage

Information
Parents of students attending MADA and MAST
Location: Baton Rouge, LA
Members:
Latest Activity: **Dec. 18, 2010**

The Parents

✉ Send Message to Group

Members

✉ Follow New Members

Discussion Forum

TEENAGERS!!! TEENAGERS!!!!!
My beloved son or daughter has turned into a teenager, what do i do?
Started by Leah Warrington Brown. **Last reply** by Tasha W

+ Start Discussion

View All

YouTube

YouTube is one of the most popular websites and can also be your schools most powerful platform. If a picture is worth a thousand words, then video must be worth a million. YouTube is now one of the first places people go to get new information. YouTube links are now showing up as top search results on Google. Web viewers are much more likely to be impressed by, and click on, a video search result, than a traditional website.

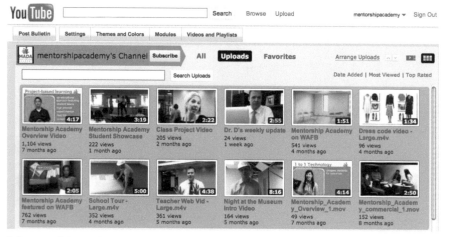

Your YouTube channel

Organize all of your uploaded videos in one place. Your YouTube channel allows you to highlight specific videos for first-time viewers. Check out our YouTube channel at youTube.com/mentorshipacademy

Upload video of school events

YouTube is a great place to feature interesting events happening at your school. Here are a few ideas of what to post:
1. Highlight reels from performing arts events
2. Sporting events such as a highlight reel of the football game
3. Interview a star student in academics, performing arts or sports
4. Feature a teacher, particularly if interviewed by a student
5. Facility updates- take a video tour of a construction project by walking around with the principal showing off the your new learning space.
6. Faculty spotlight- feature various members of your school community including cafeteria staff, paraprofessionals, and others who are not necessarily the public face of your school but have a dramatic impact on your school's operations and students.

Personal over professional

Video content that is authentic is much better than a pre-scripted professional video in the online world. For example, you can create a video from the principal's chair. It does not have to be highly edited, or contain multiple camera angles as long as the principal is authentically speaking to his or her school community. People will come to appreciate the candor of your online video.

How to record a video

Creating videos is much easier than it used to be. Most computers have a web camera built in. To create a video, simply open Windows Movie Maker or iMovie, click the camera icon and begin recording.

Video responses

An innovative way to use YouTube is to post a video response on a popular or relevant topic. For example, if your local news station posts clips of their news show on YouTube, you as the school leader can post a video response to that news story, giving your own take on the issue at hand. This is also possible on some news sites (such as CNN.com) where you can post your response to relevant articles and videos.

The more that you engage in the conversation, the more that people will associate you with professional experience. Each of your videos could have a text-based link that refers viewers back to your school website. These videos could also be posted on your blog or school website to keep the conversation going and to share your ideas with your school community.

Favorites

One great feature of your YouTube channel is the "favorites" section. You can designate other videos on YouTube as your favorites, representing your school's philosophy, supporting your school's methodology, or just showing your school's personality. Visitors to your YouTube profile will see your favorite videos and associate these videos with your school's brand.

You Tube [   ] Search   Browse   Upload

teachers hthnc music video

▶ ◀)) 0:40 / 3:19   360p ⚙ Ⓖ ▭ ↱ ⤢

👍 Like 👎 ┊   ✚ Add to ▾   Share   Embed   🚩   **2,986** ⓘ

ThePFactor   Not gonna lie... I wish I could've gone to a high school
1 year ago 3 👍   that was this cool!

Have some fun online

At the end of the school year, a team of teachers and I got together and created a music video, rewriting the lyrics to a popular song. We played the video on the screen for students at the end of a talent show. The students enjoyed the video and many wanted to watch the video again.

That evening, I posted the video on my YouTube account and was amazed by the several hundred views overnight. The video had spread like wildfire. The comments below the video were especially encouraging. This silly video for a talent show posted on YouTube brought much more attention to our school than a $3,000 radio campaign on the local radio station. YouTube is a powerful tool that everyone online uses, so consider ways to take advantage of it.

YouTube

Getting started on YouTube

Even if you only post one video, use YouTube. Start with faculty interviews. This is an easy first video to create. A question could simply be, "why do you like working at the school?" With one camera and a variety of teachers sitting behind a desk explaining their perspective. Using simple video editing programs, these videos can be cut and edited together with music and titles added for a more professional appearance.

Recruiting students with YouTube

Put yourself in the shoes of upcoming students. They want to know who their teachers are. They want to know what kind of school they might attend. By finding you on YouTube these students are going to be impressed.

Recruiting teachers with YouTube

Differentiate yourself and your school by using YouTube to recruit teachers.
1. Create a video introducing your school, touring the facilities, and highlighting why potential teachers should work at your school.
2. Post this video on YouTube and embed it on your website and craigslist.
3. Ask applicants to create their own introductory videos to be sent in before interviewing them. You'll be surprised by the results.

mentorshipacademy's Channel Subscribe   All   **Uploads**   Favorites

0:32 / 4:38   360p

Online surveys

Receiving authentic feedback and compiling the data you receive are key components of integrating social media into your school experience. Social media allows you to hear directly from your constituents, figure out what you are doing well and discover ways you can improve to better serve their needs. Although commenting is available with many of the tools already discussed, a tried and true method of receiving feedback is the survey, with free online survey tools available gathering authentic feedback from your school community has never been easier.

The purpose of a survey

Start by defining the end goal of each survey you create. There needs to be specific reason you are asking parents, students or community members to complete your survey.

Audiences and topics we've surveyed

Students- overall school experience survey to improve our systems
Parents- technology use survey to better our communication methods
Teachers- job satisfaction survey to help prevent teacher burnout
Community- mentor interest survey to encourage the community to invest in our students through personal relationships

Creating a survey

A survey creation site such as Survey Monkey or Wufoo allow you to quickly construct surveys, distribute them to the appropriate audiences and place them on your website or other social media platforms. These tools allow you to choose from several different question types, closed-ended, open-ended and likert scale questions.

Tow that you have defined the reason for your survey, you can begin constructing it. When you are constructing a survey it is best to keep it short and concise. An extremely long survey can be overwhelming to your audience, and they will not take the time to complete it.

1. Parent Technology Use Survey

2. Parents, in an effort to improve our electronic communication, please complete the surve questions listed below.

Email

3. _____

How do you prefer to be contacted by your child's teachers?

4. ⦿ Email
○ Phone
○ Letters mailed home
○ Teacher's Web sites

5.

How often do you use:	Never	Sometimes	Monthly	Weekly	Daily
Ning	○ 1	○ 2	○ 3	○ 4	○ 5
Teacher Web sites	○ 1	○ 2	○ 3	○ 4	○ 5
Engrade	○ 1	○ 2	○ 3	○ 4	○ 5
Mentorship Academy Web site	○ 1	○ 2	○ 3	○ 4	○ 5
Mentorship Academy Facebook page	○ 1	○ 2	○ 3	○ 4	○ 5

6. Submit

1. Survey title - a descriptive title can help you stay organized and communicate the purpose of the survey.

2. Survey instructions - As members of your school community may not be familiar with online surveys, instruct them through the steps.

3. Email address - When appropriate, I collect survey respondents' email addresses to allow us to share the results with them and ensure we have an accurate email on file.

4. Multiple choice question - An example multiple choice question where users can only choose one of several answer prompts..

5. Matrix question - These questions are great at measuring items on a scale such as frequency of use or satisfaction with your program.

6. Submit - One click submit and you'll have instant access to the results.

Track feedback over time

Conduct the survey at least once a month. Use the same questions to track data over time. See how you improve and what you still need to work on. Leave open-ended question to allow participants to make suggestions, connect you to other members of the community, and to vent their frustration.

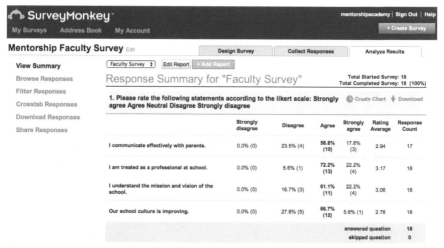

Data analysis

Survey Monkey allows you to create "Response Summaries" to view the total average responses to specific items on your survey.

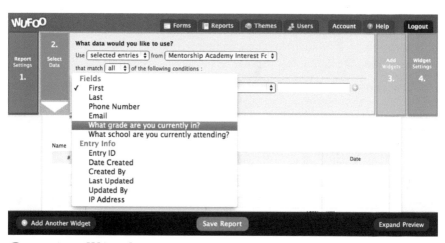

Survey filtering

Wufoo has a really simple tool for creating reports. They also make it easy to share these reports with others by sending a link to an online version.

Chart creation

Both Survey Monkey and Wufoo have dynamic chart creation tools that allow you to display specific answers, preview the chart, and publish for an audience. You can also download the source data as an .xls file to create your own charts in a spreadsheet program such as Excel.

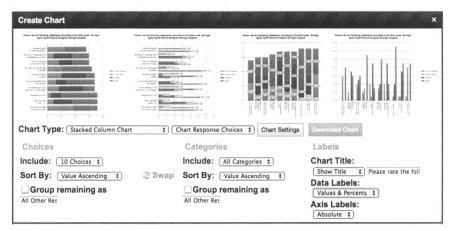

Best practices for analyzing results

1. Be sure to have enough responses for a representative sample.
2. Provide a paper version of surveys for parents without Internet access.
3. Offer an "additional comments" box to allow respondents to share their perspective on important issues not addressed in the survey or provide context to their answers.

Exporting survey data

Online survey tools allow you export all survey information and import into a spreadsheet program such as Microsoft Excel. Exporting data in this ways allows you to compile a full profile of students you are recruiting, a donor you are attempting to profile, or a community member you are attempting to engage. You are also able to integrate the downloaded data into an existing student information system with updated phone numbers and student information.

39

Email

Email can be an efficient tool in your social media toolbox. But most people do not use email efficiently. In these next few pages, we will share some email best practices that just might change the way you use email forever.

Four step email processing

1. Select All - My first step in dealing with email is to select all.

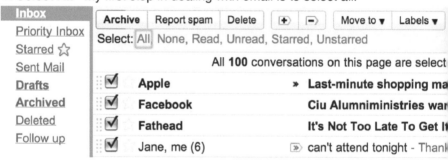

2. Star Important - I then star each important email I need to follow up on.

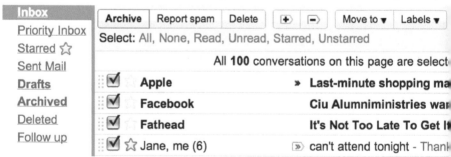

3. Archive the rest - When I click archive, all emails are moved to the archive folder. This removes them from the inbox but saves them in case I need to access them later. With the large mailbox size Gmail allows, there is no reason to delete any email message.

4. Review Stars - View the stars folder to read and respond to important email. Once you've responded, unstar the email to save to the archive folder.

Every email message that comes into your inbox must be processed for you to have an empty inbox free of unanswered email messages.

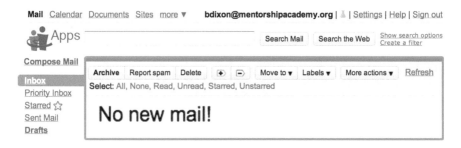

Two essential folders:

For the email that is difficult to process, there are two folders that will help you clean out your inbox.

Read someday folder - Place email messages you wold like to read when you have time in here. These may include newsletters, funny email forwards or list serve messages. Moving an email to the "read someday" folder allows you to remove the email from your inbox, but get back to it when you have time.

Waiting for folder - Once you've sent an email reply that requires a re-sponse from someone else, bcc yourself and drag this email into a "waiting for" folder. Check this folder weekly to ensure you've received responses to important issues. A simple "waiting for" tracking system will dramatically change your school's communication impact.

Take control of your inbox

Almost every school leader I've spoken to is overwhelmed by the amount of email he or she receives on a daily basis. I have found the following tips to dramatically improve the handling of my email inbox.

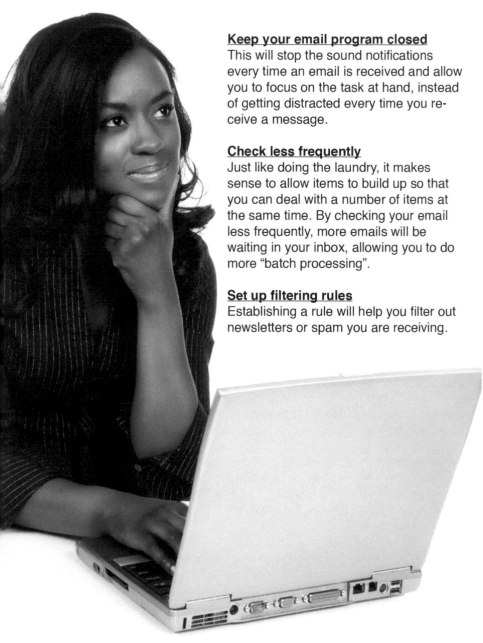

Keep your email program closed
This will stop the sound notifications every time an email is received and allow you to focus on the task at hand, instead of getting distracted every time you receive a message.

Check less frequently
Just like doing the laundry, it makes sense to allow items to build up so that you can deal with a number of items at the same time. By checking your email less frequently, more emails will be waiting in your inbox, allowing you to do more "batch processing".

Set up filtering rules
Establishing a rule will help you filter out newsletters or spam you are receiving.

Advanced Email Tips

Learning to effectively use email is an essential function of today's school leaders. Although there are more comprehensive resources available for advanced email tips, I've outlined a few key tips below including email groups, smart subjects, context-based email addresses, and a catch-all account.

Email groups

Establishing email groups can save you time when communicating to a specific audience. Although most schools have preset groups such as teachers@yourschool.org- where the email is distributed to all of the teachers at your school, you may want to create custom groups for faculty teams, community members, or professional colleagues.

How to create an email group in Gmail:
1. Click on contacts
2. Name group
3. Add email addresses to group and save
4. Test in a new message

Smart subjects

One way to better communicate through email is to use the subject line to cue the reader to your intention for sending that email. Two frequent emails I send are articles I would like the faculty to read and a meeting I want them to attend. For the article to read, I preface the subject with the words READ ONLY: NY Times article. For the meeting, I write RESPOND PLEASE: Thursday meeting. Both of these "smart subjects" help clarify the purpose of the email to help ensure the message isn't ignored or lost.

Context-based email addresses

We use specific email addresses for specific functions:
-job@mentorshipacademy.org
-forward to specific members of the committee. This can change, but you don't have to change the email address.
-facebook@mentorshipacademy.org
-universal login for multiple users to manage. You can always change the password, but don't have to change the email address to manage it.

Catch-all account

Anything sent to an incorrect email address is sent to the email adminis-trator. This way, email is never lost, but simply forwarded to the correct person.

Classroom portals

Introduction

Every class in your school should have an online portal, a place you can travel to virtually and engage the classroom learning. Though the portal may look like a blog, course website, or course management system, the approach is different. Rather than simply downloading documents or accessing the teacher's email address, a classroom portal allows a community of learning to interact with each other in an authentic way.

Features of a classroom portal

Depending on the platform, there are multiple tools to select from in building your classroom portal. At a minimum, you should consider including the following components:

Basic information

Teacher's contact information, the name of the class, online syllabus, online textbook or pdf articles, links to relevant videos are all important components for students to be able to access.

Downloadable documents

Anything that you photocopy and pass out to the class include a downloadable link on your classroom portal. This includes permission forms, articles, worksheets, even class notes. Archiving this important information will save you time in the future and allow students to have access to this in the future.

Collaboration tools

Ensuring your classroom portal becomes an online community depends on frequent use of available collaboration tools. The tools may include a discussion forum, document uploading, commenting and rating features, screen sharing, and online chat.

Benefits of a classroom portal

There are several benefits to an online classroom portal. These include collaboration, authentic assessment, increased engagement, and relevance.

Collaboration

Classroom portals change the dynamic of your class from one teacher delivering content to multiple users collaborating. Teachers and students can quickly and easily update their profile, upload documents, and respond to others' work. Many tools, such as document sharing allow groups to collaborate on a project in real-time online. Students also benefit from the feedback they receive on their work from other students, helping to shift the emphasis from the grade they will receive to the quality of work they complete.

Authentic assessment

Rather than simply relying on a weekly test or homework as your main method of assessment, a classroom portals allows you evaluate students using multiple means. A discussion forum rubric can be useful in assessing constructive contributions students have made to the class. Revision tracking helps you evaluate progress in students' writing projects. Online pre and post tests allow students to demonstrate mastery on key classroom concepts.

Increased engagement

With a classroom portal, multiple conversations can occur at the same time. Instead of every student completing the same assignment, a classroom portal allows students to build on each other's work. Students can respond to the classroom discussion, write their thoughts on the classroom reading, and give feedback on the original work of their peers all in one central location. Expressing their own viewpoint and hearing other student viewpoints increases student engagement in your course activities.

Relevance

Since the classroom portal can be updated by anyone, anywhere, what used to be static classroom content can now be made relevant. When an event happens in the news, links to the story and related videos can be posted on the classroom portal. Students can respond to these resources, allowing them to engage in the ongoing conversation the adult world is having. These activities help to course content and state standards more relevant to students, demonstrating a link between their classroom learning and the world around them.

Multiple platforms, singular focus

In today's age of free online tools, there is an overwhelming number of plat-forms to choose from for your classroom portal. My two favorite are Google Sites and Moodle.

Google Sites

Part of the free Google Apps package, including Gmail, Calendar and Documents, Google Sites is a great platform for hosting your classroom portal. Not only is Sites free, but it is easy to use. Using a "What you see is what you get" editor, updating your Google Site is as simple as using Word. Another advantage of Sites is the wealth of training resources available on-line. Finally, the integration between Sites and all of the other Google tools makes it a tool worthy of consideration.

Moodle

Similar to Blackboard or other course management software programs, Moodle is a free online platform that serves as an effective classroom portal. Although a bit more complicated than Google Sites, Moodle allows multiple users and administrators, a course calendar, online tests, discus-sion forums, and even an online gradebook. With Moodle receiving wide-spread adoption at universities across the country, Moodle is worth taking a look at.

Frequently updated

The most important aspect of a classroom portal is frequent updating. Even the most experienced teachers look like amateurs when their websites are outdated. To to stay a place of relevant information, classroom portals need to be updated at least once a week. As an example, a link to "This week's homework" needs to be updated weekly. Online tools are only effective if they are used frequently. Encourage teachers to keep their classroom por-tal updated by reviewing it with them during your regular meetings.

Classroom portals

Postcard page

Being aware of the high percentage of "technophobic teachers" still teaching in the classroom, it may be unrealistic to expect every teacher to manage their own online classroom portal. To counter the problem of outdated websites, each teacher should start by creating a static "postcard page". This serves as the first page a visitor views and features content that does not require frequent updating. From this postcard page, visitors would then click on to the classroom portal.

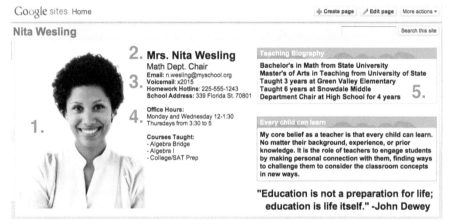

An example postcard page

1. Your picture - Establish a personal connection with visitors by posting an updated picture of yourself. Parents and students will recognize you on the first day, helping to build that important relationship.

2. Your name - Obviously the most important part of the site for first time visitors.

3. Contact information - Ensure visitors can communicate with you by including your email address, telephone extension, homework hotline number, and school address.

4. Office hours - Make it easy for parents to set up a conference with you by posting the times you are available for meetings.

5. Professional information - Help visitors get to know you by posting a brief biography, a short professional resume outlining your experience, and a few sentences on your educational philosophy.

Student portfolios

In today's competitive online world, each of your students should create and manage their own online portfolio highlighting their best schoolwork.

○ ○ ○   My Student Portfolio

◄ ► + https://sites.google.com/a/mentorshipacademy.org/example-student/   ↻

Thomas Ryland

Search this site

Biography
Career Goals
College Plan
Resume
School Projects
Sitemap

Welcome to my Digital Portfolio.

Here you will learn about me, view my projects, and understand my goals for life.

Sign in   Recent Site Activity   Terms   Report Abuse   Print page | Powered by Google Sites

Benefits of online student portfolios

1. Prepares for college and career applications

Online portfolios are more impressive than traditional resumes. College admissions counselors love to see student work when choosing between applicants. Placing a web address of an online portfolio on their resume, students are more likely to stand apart from the crowd when applying for a scholarship, internship, or career position.

2. Student engagement and expression

When schools utilize student portfolios, they see an increased level of student engagement. Student work becomes more valuable when students know that others will be viewing their work. When students are able to choose their best work to share with the larger community, they put forth increased effort in completing that work.

3. Familiar tools

Portfolio platforms such as Google sites allow students to keep their portfolios updated using familiar tools. What once required complex web programing is now as easy as saving a Word document. Many platforms also allow students to link their social media accounts to their portfolio, allowing the content to stay updated automatically.

School-based best practices
1. Educate students on the value of an online portfolio.
Strategies for teaching students the importance of their online portfolio include:
-College freshman talking about how their own portfolios help them in their college admissions process
-Students viewing the online portfolios of professionals in their field
-Hosting a dialogue with college admissions counselors emphasizing the importance of student portfolios

2. Frequent updating
Portfolios are a work in progress. Outdated content can quickly lead to disengagement by the portfolio viewer and the student himself. Make updating student portfolios part of your weekly class schedule.

Name: _Chris_   Comments:

Content: 1   2   ③   4   *missing contact info*

Content: 1   ②   3   4   *outdated work*

Content: 1   2   3   ④   *the pages go together*

Content: 1   2   3   ④   *the design is professional*

3. Frequent presentation and feedback
Hold students accountable for updating their online portfolios by having them present their portfolios once a month to the class. They should have something new to share each time they present. Allow other students to give their feedback and suggestions (Use the feedback form above as an example). Rotate students through a daily portfolio presentation, with one student updating the class on his/ her portfolio progress each and every day.

4. Frequent assessment
Create a school-wide rubric to set clear expectations of students' online portfolios. Consider implementing an online portfolio grade for every grading period. By frequently assessing student portfolios, students will continuously update their portfolio content.

Technology tips
1. Function over fashion.
Although there are more professional applications, such as Wordpress and Drupal, we use Google Sites for our online portfolio system. Sites is easy to use and has many templates to get you started. With simple tools like Google Sites, students can easily update their portfolio with recent work without extensive tech knowledge.

2. Leverage training resources
No matter what system you use, ensure students have access to training resources. With Google Sites, many students will be able to get started without any technology training. Google Sites and Wordpress do have training tools available online such video tutorials, forums, and user guides when a student needs help or wants to explore advanced features.

3. Manage users
When implementing an online portfolio system, ensure you are able to perform basic administrative functions. From our experience, you will need to frequently register new users, remove inappropriate content, and reset user passwords. Instead of having students sign up for a website that you're not an administrator of, such as Webs.com or Blogger, Google Sites allows you to perform administrative functions across your school network.

Getting started

1. Visit the online portfolios of several schools

Just Google "student online portfolios" to visit example portfolios to share with your students.

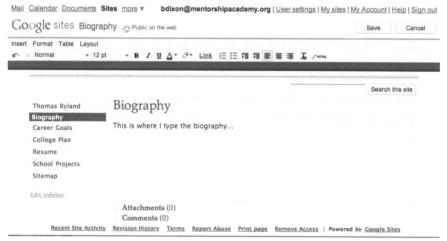

2. Create your own online portfolio

Learn from experience by signing up for Google Sites. Start using your site to communicate your daily class agenda or homework to students. You'll be surprised at how easy it is to use.

3. Going deeper

Look at the online portfolios of artists in your area. Consider the many ways that you can utilize the best practices to help engage the students. Contact them to present their work to your school community.

Showcasing students, showcasing your school

Online portfolios serve as dynamic student recruiting tools. When a prospective students visits your school's website and those portfolios are of a high quality, those upcoming students will be inspired, imagining themselves in the shoes of a current student. Posting links to student portfolios on your website can help prospective students be better informed about your school experience.

School leader's blog

Why Blog?

The school leader is the chief representative of your school's brand. Regular communication from the head of school is necessary for keeping your school community informed and engaged. In an age of Twitter and Podcasting, weekly newsletters are no longer good enough. The leader of the school needs to utilize today's technology to accomplish the authentic communication expected in our connected world.

Begin the conversation

A simple blog is a good place to start. Using blogger or wordpress, you can have a professional looking blog online and updated in just a few minutes.

What do you blog about?

Even if you feel that you do not have anything interesting to say online, remember, you are the school leader. Your students, teachers, parents, and community want to hear from your viewpoint on variety of topics.

Here are a few suggestions to get you started:

-Answering frequently asked questions
-Making announcements
-Sharing highlights of past events
-Asking questions to the community
-Sharing ideas about education
-An interactive book talk

Best practices

Professional

Make it look professional. Start with a blog on Wordpress.com and take advantage of the many templates.

A gorgeously minimal two-column theme with a flexible layout and an unusual blue color scheme.

A dark, elegant one-column theme with a widget-ready footer. Options include a custom header image, custom background

A beautiful and colorful theme that can be further customized with support for custom menus, background, and header.

This light and colorful theme provides a beautiful backdrop for your WordPress site with delicate, hand-drawn illustrations.

Updated

Keep it updated. The worst thing you can do is to post once or twice and never touch it again. People will expect you to update your content.

Authentic

Although your blog is a great opportunity to engage your school community in an authentic way, remember that what you say will be seen as representing your school. Be sure to avoid politics, controversial personal opinions, or anything else that might get you into hot water. The best approach is to focus on your school, sharing your perspective on matters that effect your school community.

Accessible

Make your content accessible to anyone who wants to stay informed by posting on multiple platforms. The easiest way to do this is to use a multi-posting service such as ping.fm or TubeMogul which automatically distributes your content to multiple platforms with only one upload.

Searchable

Use specific keywords when posting content to allow web visitors interested in the topic to quickly find your content. Tagging your videos in this way helps to spread your content across the web, assisting other school leaders and building your reputation as an expert in the field.

Use video to engage your students

Video can be used to communicate more authentically with your students. Consider starting a principal video blog where you answer questions sent in by students. Of course you can filter questions for appropriateness. When you respond to questions that they've sent in, students will feel that you are listening. Believe it or not, students will actually watch your videos.

An example is a letter I recently sent home to all of our parents. We handed the letter to the students to bring home, so we new that they would likely read it.

Since much of what we said in the letter effected them, I created a three minute video, one take, no edits, recorded on my computer's web camera explaining the content of the letter in a fun and candid way. I sent the You-Tube link to all of the teachers asking them to show it to students in the last ten minutes of class on a Friday afternoon.

They watched the video in class and all of the students felt like I had spoken directly to them. Walking the halls at the end of the day, students came up to me and asked specific questions about what I mentioned in the video. I was listening to them, and they felt that I cared.

School leader's blog

Next level leadership

Every principal must manage their personal brand. Positions come and go, but your career will last for a while, so use your current position and influence to build a personal brand that expands beyond your current school. Your content, particularly in a blog helps you build your reputation in the community. Not only does your blog help your school because you are communicating to your schools main stakeholders, but it will also have an impact on your future career.

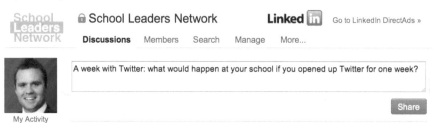

Linked in

Consider creating a group on Linked in to start a dialogue in your field. Linked in is a widely accepted tool for building your professional network.

YouTube

Posting regular video clips on YouTube will help establish your standing as an expert in your field. The more views your videos receive, the more impact you'll have on the topic you are focusing on in your video.

Cell phones

Innovative school leaders use their cell phones to have authentic, ongoing conversations with the school community. In an age of email and cell phones, people are much more accessible than they used to be. Embracing your cell phone as tool to engage with your school community can help you be a more communicative school leader and take your use of social media to the next level.

Update Facebook "On the Go"

Most smart phones now have a Facebook app that allows you to update your school's Facebook page on the go. I frequently update our school's Facebook page with pictures of school activities while making my daily rounds.

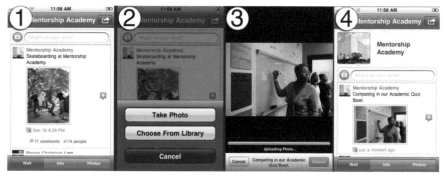

1. Open the Facebook app and search for your school's page.
2. Click "take photo".
3. Upload the photo and add a description.
4. Review your updated page.

Collaborating with parents

Of course the cell phone is no longer just for voice communication, but for text messaging and photo sharing and now even video. School principals are beginning to find that text messaging is a great tool for establishing contact with parents. When dealing with student issues, I prefer to call parents on their cell phone. After the conversation, I send a quick thank you text and add the parent to my contacts. I'll likely need this number in the future. Parents may not answer their phones will at work, but they may be able to read a text. There are even systems available now that allow you to send a mass text message to all cell phones in your student database.

Your personal cell phone number

Consider giving out your personal cell phone number. Numbers you don't recognize can be sent to voicemail. By allowing families to leave messages on your cell phone, you'll be able to hear directly from your constituents. You can enter their information in your phone in case you need to contact them in the future.

A personal approach

On my email signature and business card, I have my cellphone number. I believe that I work for my students and their families. It is therefore important that they contact me directly when necessary.

Families understand that this is my personal cell phone number and reluctant to call it unless it is absolutely necessary. On average, I only get a few phone calls on that phone per day. Most of these calls I would have needed to handle anyway. By giving out my personal cell phone number, families feel like they have a voice and a personal connection to the school leader.

Voicemail hotline

If giving out your personal cell phone number makes you nervous, consider setting up a voicemail hotline. A voicemail hotline allows you to hear directly from the people that you serve and helps you receive the direct feedback you need to continually improve your school. Advantages of establishing a voicemail hotline include:

1. Never rings to an actual phone:
Families can leave messages at any time without worrying about someone answering the phone.

2. Emails the voice mail audio file to you:
No need to log on to a web site or be at your computer to check your messages. They are automatically sent to you.

3. Records the sender's phone number:
Phone numbers are captured for responding to the sender.

4. Cost effective:
Establishing a voicemail hotline is far cheaper than setting up another cell phone to handle parent phone calls to a school number.

Setting up a voicemail hotline

Two options for setting up your own voicemail hotline are Skype and K7. Skype is a web-based alternative to a traditional telephone. K7 is a free service that allows you to set up an inbound voicemail box. Both options forward your voicemail messages to your email inbox, allowing you to listen to the messages at your computer or on your smart phone.

Skype

Skype's Online Number service allows you to create a local phone number with online voicemail for less than ten dollars a month. Visit skype.com to learn more.

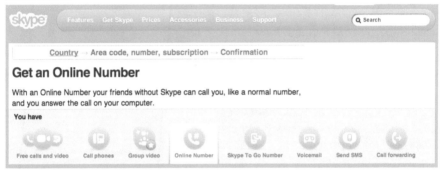

K7.net

A free alternative to Skype's online voicemail is K7.net. You can sign up for a telephone number with a Seattle-based area code. When families call your number, your custom greeting plays and they can leave you a message.

Either one of these options give families the feeling that they are being listened to. It also allows you to have much more authentic conversations with them and eliminates some of the gatekeepers preventing you from truly knowing the cares and concerns of your students and parents. A voicemail hotline allows you to be in tune with your school community.

Text-message marketing

Another effective tool for engaging your school community is text messaging. One of our more effective text-messaging tools has been textmarks. On our postcard, we tell those interested to text "mentorship" to 41411 for more information. They receive a special message back on their phone almost instantly. The service also keeps a log of the numbers of respondents so that we can follow up.

Mobile polling

Although most schools have banned the use of cell phones by students, we have found at least one effective way to use these "pocket computers" as tools for receiving instant feedback from our students. In a school assembly, we conduct a live poll using multiple-choice questions where students can text in their vote. Poll everywhere is a tool lets your community use their cell phone to text in responses to survey questions.

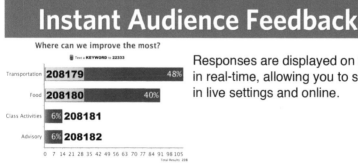

Responses are displayed on the webpage in real-time, allowing you to share results in live settings and online.

Your online presence

It doesn't matter how great your online content is if your target audience cannot locate you online. Building your "online presence" helps position your content in a way that is easy to find. Three tools to help your school build its online presence are Google Places, Namechk, and Ping.fm.

Google Places

Listing your school on Google is one of the most effective ways to build your online presence. Google Places is a tool for business to integrate with Google Maps. By listing your school's address, contact information, and brief description with Google Places, your school will appear near the top of the results when someone searches for it.

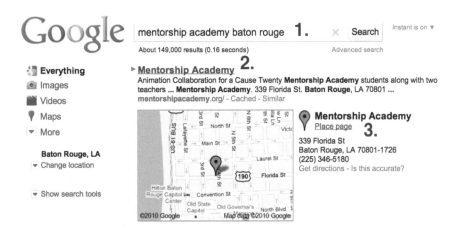

Your Google search results

Begin by searching for your school name and city on Google. The results will give you a picture of what visitors see when they search for your school. Let's look at the results of my search above.

1. Search terms - These are the terms I searched for. Try adding your city name or other identifying details your community might include.

2. Your webpage summary - With a search engine optimized page (SEO), your school should be the first result that shows up.

3. Google map results - We listed our school with Google Places to ensure community members have access to directions and contact information. To set up your school, visit: **google.com/places**

Namechk.com

Sign up for multiple social media services just in case members of your audience use that service. Namechk let's you see if your desired username or vanity url is still available at dozens of popular Social Networking and Social Bookmarking websites. Register your school name on the most popular sites to ensure your audience can find your content.

Ping.fm

Now that you're set up on multiple social networks, use a service such as Ping.fm to automatically post updates across all networks. Linking accounts is a simple process.

Getting started with Ping.fm

1. Sign up for multiple networks - Ensure you have the username and password for sites such as Facebook and Twitter. We use one email address and a unified password for our social networks.

2. Create an account on Ping.fm - The email is key here. We created ping@mentorshipacademy.org to make it easy.

3. Set-up multiple posting - Connect all of your networks to start pinging!

An example event

To help bring all of the social media tools together, let's use a recent "Service Learning Day" we had at our school as an example of how we actually implement our Social Media strategies.

The school-wide events

We partnered with 11 non-profits in the Greater Baton Rouge area to create a service-learning opportunity for our students. Here is how we used social media before, during, and after the day to keep families and the community included in the conversation.

The social media tools

Below you will find the many ways we used the twelve social media tools discussed in this book before, during, and after our service day. Our strategy is outlined below with tools highlighted for reference.

Before assigning students to non-profits, we used an **online survey** to gauge student interest in specific causes. This helped us know which non-profits to reach out to based on student interest. We could have also created a survey for non-profits learning about their interest level in having our students volunteer.

Our initial **email** to the selected non-profits included some basic information about our school as well as links to our **website** and **social media pages**. This allowed us to establish credibility with these potential partners, who were then able to learn much more about our school through photos, videos, articles, and status updates on our social media pages.

Once the volunteer opportunities were setup, we began to promote the Service-Learning Day. We started by announcing the event in our weekly **e-newsletter** to families. We posted a link to this **e-newsletter** on the front page of our **website**. We posted the date of the event with Ping.fm, automatically updating all of our networks including **Facebook** and **twitter**.

We began a discussion topic on **Ning** to get students excited for the event and to get their feedback. Students also created a "service learning" section on their **student portfolio** to being blogging about the event.

As the school leader, I created a video about the service learning day and posted on my **blog** and **YouTube** account.

One tool, many uses

Of all the tools in our social media toolbox, Facebook has been the most effective. Below you'll find three ways we used Facebook for this event.

1. Before the event, post the announcement

 Mentorship Academy All Mentorship students and teachers volunteering at 11 community organizations today!
October 15 at 11:06am · Comment · Like · Share · Promote

👍 3 people like this.

 Gloria Chapman Good Luck......
October 15 at 11:24am · Like · Flag

2. During the event, post pictures and updates

 Mentorship Academy Students and teachers volunteering at St. Vincent de Paul Center

📷 October 15 at 12:06pm · Comment · Like · Share

👍 2 people like this.

3. After the event, post links to online media

 Mentorship Academy Mentorship Academy Service Learning Day

 **Oct 16, 2010 12:05am**
Length: 0:46

🎥 October 16 at 12:05am · Comment · Like · Share

👍 5 people like this.

 DeVora Knight Robinson Mentorship Academy doing it right. I'm glad my son attends there. FYI tha's him in the yellow sweatshirt helping to pack the boxes at the food bank. I love how during intersession the kids have to volunteer in the community on the last day of intersession.
October 16 at 9:57am · Like · Flag

From traditional media to social media

Don't forget to use traditional media, such as TV news and printed news-papers, to tell your school's story. These outlets can be great sources of content for posting to your social media networks.

Capture and repurpose the coverage

Having a story about our school run on TV or in the newspaper is only the first step. Here's how to convert a news spot to a video on your website to ensure your school community will be able to watch the coverage later.

From offline...

First, use iRecord, a personal media recorder that records video and audio onto a USB drive from your TV, to record the local newscast.

To online...

Next, plug the USB stick into a computer and upload the video onto your YouTube account for your subscribers to watch and other viewers to find.

To our website...

Once the video footage from local newscasts are on You-Tube, use the "embed codes" to post the media onto your school website.

4B ■ Saturday, October 16, 2010 ■ The Advocate

Charter school students learn service

BY CHARLES LUSSIER
Advocate staff writer

Fourteen ninth-grade girls skipped the cafeteria at their school Friday and instead helped serve lunch to hundreds of adults who can't afford a meal of their own.

These students from the new charter school, the Mentorship Academy, were volunteering at the Society of St. Vincent de Paul's cafeteria near downtown Baton Rouge.

The school — it's actually two small high schools in one — sent its more than 250 ninth-graders to 12 different locations, involving 11 different organizations, most of them nonprofit groups.

Such service-learning days are common at many high schools. In the case of the Mentorship Academy, which opened in July, it's the second such day; students spent a day in July fixing up Lanier Elementary.

"It's such a great opportunity," said Kelley McCormick, the school's communications coordinator. "I think it's something they're going to remember."

Advocate photo by **APRIL BUFFINGTON**

Quineshia Charles, 14, a student at the Mentorship Academy, brings a plate to someone who was unable to stand in line Friday at St. Vincent de Paul. Charles was one of 250 ninth-graders from the academy to take part in a service-learning day, which had students at 12 locations.

Newspaper clipping courtesy of Baton Rouge Advocate- 2theadvocate.com

Say "Thank you"
Don't forget to send a thank you note to the reporter when your story runs. The key is to develop a long term, trusting relationship with the media.

Don't forget to reflect
To finish our service learning day, I asked all of the students to email me their reflections on the day. It was a great way to continue the conversation and build relationships with a number of students at our school.

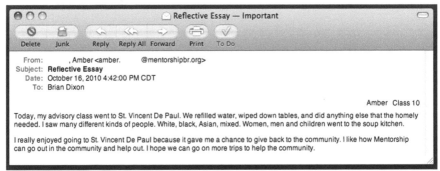

Where to begin

Getting started

Hopefully this guide has inspired you to get started on your social media journey. As a parting word, here are a few success principles we have discovered to ensure your venture into the world of social media is not short lived. The success principles include start small, delegate, and frequently assess.

Start small

A key principle to a successful social media strategy is to start small. Focus on only two tools to begin. Facebook and Google Places.
Facebook has been our most effective tool. Google Places helps new visitors find your school both in person and online.

Facebook:
Log on to Facebook and create your school's Fan page. Start with the basic information, and then begin adding more media rich content such a photo albums and videos.

Google Places:
Visit google.com/place to make sure your school can be found on Google Maps.

Delegate

Although many people contribute, it is of the utmost importance to have one person manage your social media. We created a "communications coordinator" position to manage these tools. She has a daily process for posting updated stories about our school, updating the newsletter and website, updating our FaceBook and Twitter, and managing feedback received through any of our multiple channels. If you are unable to create this type of position, share the responsibility among your administration, teachers, and office staff. Even the students can be a big help!

Frequently assess

Establish a "social media team" that meets regularly.
        -include representatives (students, teachers, parents, admin)
        -review recent posts
        -assign shared responsibility
        -look at upcoming tools
Remember "what gets measured, gets managed". A regular check-up meeting will ensure your social media strategy is properly executed.

The principal's daily picture

One great place to start is by taking and uploading a daily picture. While doing your regular classroom rounds, take out your cell phone and take a picture of what you see. A student presentation, a guest speaker, and student work are always great content for posting. Add your own comment to the picture before posting. Your school community will begin to expect and look forward to viewing your daily update. And the best part is that it takes less than a minute each day.

Next steps

Setting up your networks and steps to begin:

Twitter:
Create your school's Twitter account. Remember to use only 140 characters to get your message out. Post updates daily.

YouTube:
Create and personalize your school's YouTube Channel. Click upload, then "record from webcam" to record your first video.

Ning:
Create a school-wide Ning network at ning.com. Invite your faculty to an online discussion forum.

Daily habits that make a big difference

An effective way to begin a new routine is to ensure you participate in it every single day for at least 20 days in a row. Chose one social media strategy and implement it every day for four consecutive weeks of school. Set a daily alarm to remind you.

Internet safety

When talking about social media, we'd be remiss not to mention the concern many principals have over student safety. The Internet has changed the way students socialize and communicate with each other. Rumors and gossip have changed from the passing of notes in class to the public posting of vicious comments on Facebook.

The dangers outlined

Today's school administrators are dealing with these issues regularly:
1. Students recording videos or taking pictures of the mentally disabled and posting them on YouTube for others to laugh at.
2. Students secretly recording "teacher rants" or less than professional teacher behavior.
3. Inappropriate messaging between teachers and students via unmonitored social technology including Facebook and email.
4. Sexting: students sending explicit pictures or text from their cell phones, often occurring on school campus during the school day.

With these considerable legal issues, it is understandable why school officials would want to avoid social media altogether. Many schools have an outright ban on cell phones on campus and have implemented strict firewalls blocking YouTube and Facebook. But the reality is, social media is here to stay. Savvy school administrators need to adopt effective strategies to help manage the issues arising from the use of the tools and continue to find ways to utilize these tools for student learning.

Consider the deep and rich learning applications of social technology including collaboration, student creation, peer review, revision, personal expression, audience interactions, and real-world connections.

Six Safety Steps

Here are five specific steps schools can take to educate students and parents to utilize social media safely and effectively:

1. Start small
Start with one technology, perhaps student portfolios. It can be tempting to dive into the deep end of social media but this would be foolish.

2. Get trained
When adopting new technology, ensure that students and teachers have adequate training. Knowing a tool well will help ensure the focus stays on learning.

3. Teach parents
Empower your parents by hosting an Internet Safety seminar. An effective speaker will teach parents about the dangers online and answer questions they have.

Safe on Facebook DVD
available at brianjdixon.com

4. Hire a great faculty
Hire a competent and student-centered director of technology. It is important that your technology staff be both experts in the technology but also love working with students. The purpose of technology at school is not to catch students breaking rules, but to educate them to use technology wisely in a safe environment. Since there is no 100% failproof system, a student-centered staff will take the time to train teachers, talk to kids, and collaborate with parents when things go awry.

5. Utilize group policing
When inappropriate content is posted, and it will be posted, the community of users is empowered to flag the content. On Ning, for example, all of our teachers are administrators and students have the opportunity to flag inappropriate content, reporting it to an administrator.

6. Build a culture of collaboration.
Students need to feel that they can report what is happening online, particularly when a situation has gotten out of control. With students feeling such a personal connection to their computer, it can feel like a violation to report to the school administration. Find ways to build a culture of trust.

Resource Guide

Now that you have read this book, the following resources
may be of interest to you. All are available on brianjdixon.com

**My Empty Inbox: Avoid Email Overload
and Get Things Done**

This video guide teaches you how to:
Overcome Email Overload.
Limit Incoming Email
Set Up Your System
Clean Up Your Inbox
Prevent Email Build-Up
Improve Email Efficiency

**Teacher's Video Guide to using the
iPhone in the Classroom**

This video features 8 ways for the
classroom teacher to use the iPhone,
Android, Blackberry, or any other
smart phone in their daily practice.

Hiring Great Teachers: video guide

This video teaches school administrators and district personnel 12 keys to
hiring great teachers.

Yes,

I would like to receive information regarding additional training in social media techniques.

Please send me the following information:

___ information on in-person workshops.
___ information on attending a conference.
___ information on personal coaching.

Name: _____

School: _____

Email: _____

Phone: _____

mail to:

Dr. Brian J. Dixon
Mentorship Academy
339 Florida St.
Baton Rouge, LA 70801

postage
here

Response Postcard

social media

Notes:

Notes:

CPSIA information can be obtained
at www.ICGtesting.com
Printed in the USA
LVHW071318010719
622864LV00010B/313/P